KW-051-990

WHATEVER HAPPENED

TO...

THE ANCIENT GREEKS?

BY KIRSTY HOLMES

Marino Branch
Brainse Marino
Tel: 8336297

BookLife
PUBLISHING

©2019
BookLife Publishing Ltd.
King's Lynn
Norfolk, PE30 4LS

All rights reserved.
Printed in Malaysia.

A catalogue record for this
book is available from the
British Library.

ISBN: 978-1-78637-885-9

Written by:
Kirsty Holmes

Edited by:
John Wood

Designed by:
Dan Scase

All facts, statistics, web addresses
and URLs in this book were verified
as valid and accurate at time of
writing.

No responsibility for any changes
to external websites or references
can be accepted by either the author
or publisher.

BC AND AD

In this book, you will see **BC** after and **AD** before some dates.
And some of the dates might look backwards. What's going on?

AD stands for **Anno Domini** and that means 'in the year of the lord'.
Christian calendars count forwards from the year that Christians believe Jesus
Christ was born. When you see AD, you are counting forwards on the timeline.
AD 1750 = 1750 years after Jesus was born.

BC stands for **Before Christ**. If you see this next to a date, it means this happened
before the birth of Jesus Christ. When you see BC, you are counting backwards on
the timeline.
1750 BC = 1750 years before Jesus was born.

When describing a range of dates, you always count forwards. So "between 1500
and 500 BC" or "from AD 500 to AD 1500" is correct.

Check back here if you need to.

JESUS

2000
BC

1500
BC

1000
BC

500
BC

WRITE THE
YEAR AND
THEN BC

CONTENTS

Words that look like **THIS** are explained in the glossary on pages 30 and 31.

BORN

AD 500   AD 1000   AD 1500   AD 2000

WRITE AD AND THEN THE YEAR

WHATEVER HAPPENED TO THE ANCIENT GREEKS?

Imagine ancient Greece. Are you picturing lots of clever people in **TOGAS**, eating olives in the shadow of Mount Olympus? Sounds like ancient Greece to me! But if you went to Greece today, you wouldn't see Zeus on top of Mount Olympus, and you wouldn't be able to talk **PHILOSOPHY** with wise old dudes such as Aristotle. But why is that? Where did the **CULTURE**, people and traditions of one of the world's most **ICONIC** civilisations go?

YO! I'M DIONYSUS, GREEK GOD OF THE PAR-TAAY! HEY! WHERE DID EVERYBODY GO? IS THE PARTY OVER?

di0nysus
Athens

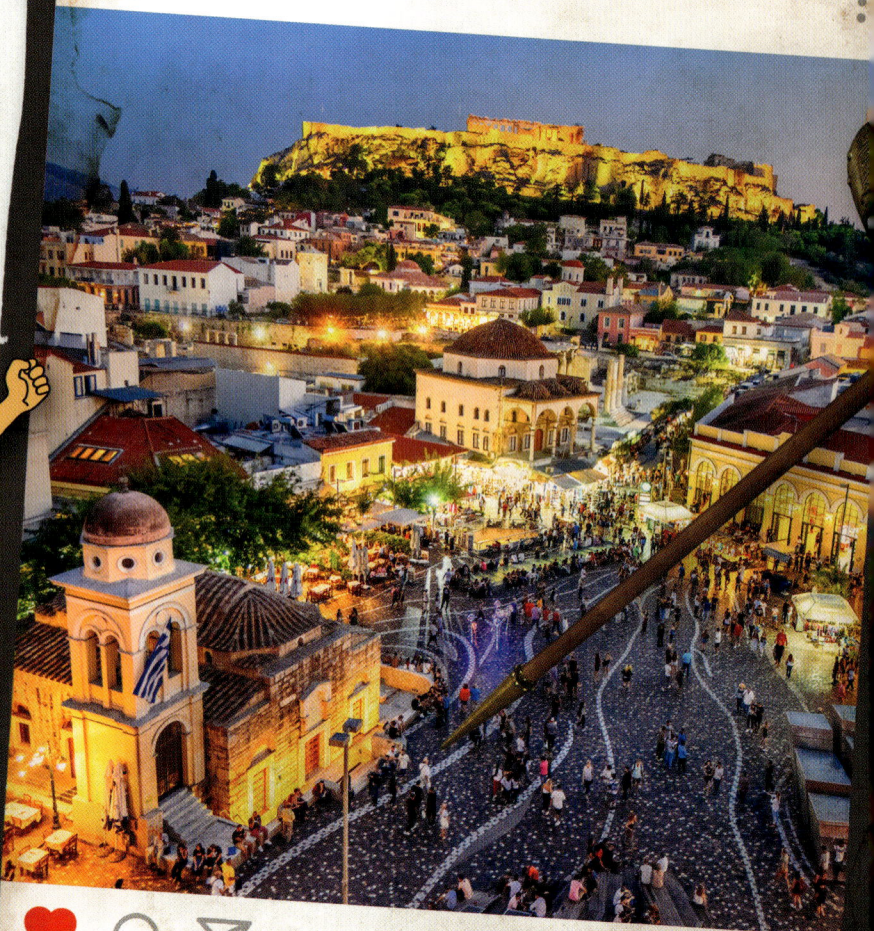

♥ **10,238 likes**

1st day in #Athens and so far, haven't seen a single god or goddess. There were no #minotaurs in the maze and everyone is wearing #ShortsNotTogas #WhateverHappenedToTheAncientGreeks #WhereDidTheyGo #ZeusAreYouThere

Show all comments (301)

2 HOURS AGO

Marino Branch
Brainse Marino
Tel: 8336297

GREEK __HOPLITES__ ARE THE BEST SOLDIERS AROUND! WE'RE UNBEATABLE! RAAAR!!

OUT WITH THE OLD AND IN WITH THE NEW

It's easy to forget that ancient peoples were just like us in many ways. They had families, jobs, homes and leaders, just like we do. But life as they knew it then was very different than life as we know it now. I bet you don't think you'll become a hoplite when you leave school — and I wonder what the ancient Greeks would have thought about our modern world? In this book, we will take a look at how the world of ancient Greece ended, and where all those things might have gone...

WAIT, WHAT? TO PRONOUNCE THESE WORDS, SAY:

PHILOSOPHY = FILL-OSS-OA-FEE

ARISTOTLE = A-RIS-TOT-UL

TURN THE PAGES OF HISTORY!

WHO WERE THE ANCIENT GREEKS?

WHERE ON EARTH?

Ancient Greece wasn't really one country. It was a collection of **CITY-STATES**, each with their own government and rules.

ANCIENT GREEKS WERE FAMOUS FOR BEING:

Thinkers
Warriors
Athletes
ARCHITECTS
POLITICIANS

Greece

...every end does not appear with its beginning...

...the only good is knowledge...

...great things are won by great dangers...

... eggs, milk, olives, bread...

OH, GODS!

The Greeks believed that the gods and goddesses were **IMMORTAL** beings who lived on Mount Olympus and watched over their lives. The gods were very powerful, and sometimes would get involved in human lives. Each god or goddess was in charge of a different thing.

SOCIAL SUCCESS

The ancient Greeks had a clear social structure, with the gods at the top and slaves at the bottom. Below is the social structure of the men of Athens. Only men from the upper classes were considered citizens, and women took their social class from their fathers and then later their husbands.

THE GODS

THE POLITES
The Upper Classes
Free men
Citizens of Athens
Born in the Athens city-state
Allowed to vote
Allowed to be politicians

THE METICS
The Middle Classes
Free men
Outsiders and foreigners
Not citizens
Traders & craftsmen
Not allowed to own houses or land
Not allowed to vote

SLAVES
Not free
Not citizens

CLASSICAL GREECE

DEMOKRATIA

Around 500 **BC**, the **P**ersian **W**ars were over, and **A**thens had become the most powerful of the city-states. In 507 **BC**, a nobleman called **C**leisthenes invented a new system to govern the state, called demokratia. The **A**ssembly was created, and any male citizen over 18 could join. Members of the **A**ssembly could vote on important things and have a say in how **A**thens was run.

PARTHENON

BUILD IT OVER THERE, ON THAT HILL. AND MAKE IT HUGE!

ACROPOLIS NOW

This was a golden age of ancient Athens. Athenian statesman Pericles ordered his architects to build an amazing temple on the hill in Athens known as the Acropolis. The temple was called the Parthenon and it really showed off how well the state of Athens was doing.

Some of the most important historians, scientists and thinkers of the Western world were born during this ERA of Greek history.

As I said in my very famous play, Antigone, "A city which belongs to just one man is no city at all."

SOPHOCLES

Archimedes was a Greek mathematician. When he was sitting in the bath one day, he figured out something important about how things float, and some people say he was so excited that he shouted "Eureka!" and ran down the street completely naked!

I'm Hippocrates. They call me the Father of Western Medicine. Even doctors now, in your modern times, take an OATH that they call the Hippocratic Oath!

WAIT, WHAT?
TO PRONOUNCE THESE WORDS, SAY:
CLEISTHENES = CLISE-THUN-EEZ
ANTIGONE = ANN-TIGGER-NEE
PERICLES = PERRY-CLEEZ
ACROPOLIS = A-CROP-UH-LISS
ARCHIMEDES = ARK-E-MEE-DEEZ
EUREKA = YUE-REEK-A
HIPPOCRATES = HIP-OK-RAT-EEZ

9

HERE COME THE POLEIS

DON'T CALL ME A GREEK. I. AM. SPARTAN!

Classical Greece may have been one of the greatest European civilisations ever, but it wasn't a **UNITED** country just yet. The city-states were like small countries of their own. There wasn't a government to tie all the big cities together, so the little towns and villages were governed by the nearest big city instead. Most Greek people would not even have called themselves Greek. They would have thought of themselves as part of the city-state they were from.

The people of the city-states had a lot in common. They all worshipped the same gods, spoke the same language, and shared many things from their culture. They probably should have been peaceful and happy... so where did it all go wrong?

ARCHAEOLOGISTS, LIKE THIS ONE, STUDY RUINS AND <u>ARTEFACTS</u> TO FIND OUT ABOUT THE ANCIENT GREEKS.

I STUDY THE WRITINGS AND THEORIES OF ANCIENT GREECE. I'M A CLASSICIST.

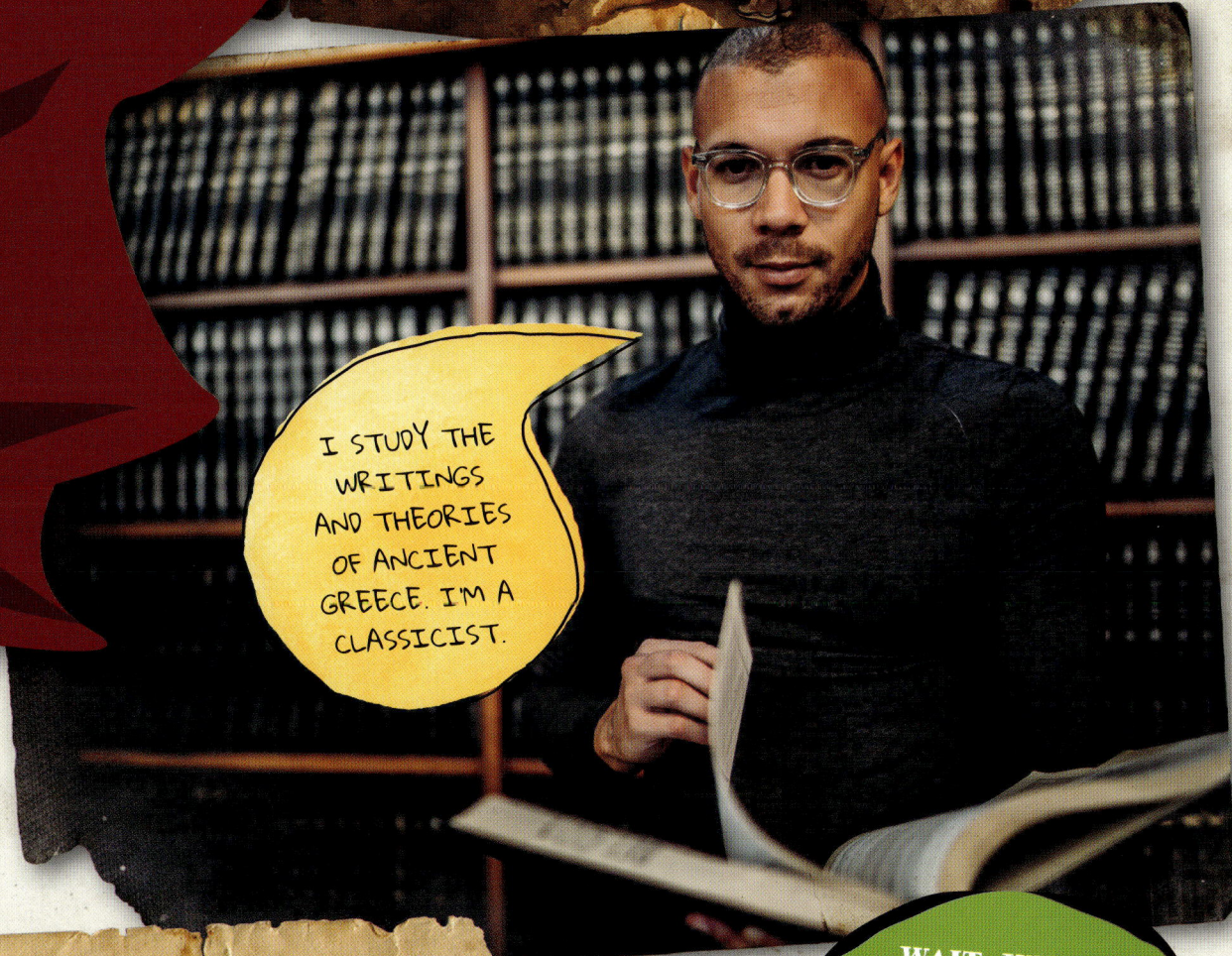

We're going to look at the story of the slow fall of one of humanity's greatest-ever civilisations. And at the end, you can make up your own mind as to why it fell.

WAIT, WHAT?
TO PRONOUNCE THESE WORDS, SAY:

ARCHAEOLOGIST =
ARK-EE-OLLO-JIST

CLASSICIST =
KLASS-ISS-IST

THE PELOPONNESIAN WARS

460–446 BC

By 460 BC, two city-states had become bigger and more powerful than the rest: Athens and Sparta. Most of the other city-states had **ALLIANCES** with either Athens or Sparta, and Greek civilisation had almost been split in two. War broke out between Athens and one of the city-states linked to Sparta. The Spartans had to defend their allies and the two giants of Greece were head-to-head. This was known as the First Peloponnesian War.

> ME AGAIN! PERICLES! WE'VE BEEN AT WAR WITH MOST OF OUR NEIGHBOURS FOR YEARS NOW, BUT THOSE SPARTANS ARE JUST THE WORST. THEY ARE SO ANGRY ALL THE TIME! WE'LL SHOW THEM WHO'S BOSS! ATHENS RULES THE SEAS!

WE SPARTANS CAN SEE THAT THE ATHENIANS THINK THEY'RE BETTER THAN US, BUT WE'RE NOT AFRAID OF THEM! WE'RE NOT GOING TO LET THE ATHENIANS FORGET ABOUT US, AND WE HEAR THEY'VE SENT TROOPS TO EGYPT TOO. PRETTY SOON, THEY'LL BE READY FOR A <u>TRUCE</u>, AND SPARTANS CAN BE VERY PATIENT.

Athens had become very powerful, and had built a lot of battleships so they had the stronger <u>NAVY</u>. Spartan people were trained as warriors from childhood; men, women and children were all fierce fighters. The Spartans had the better <u>ARMY</u>. As both city-states became larger and stronger, they made alliances with their neighbours. When Athens and Corinth started fighting over their neighbour city-state, Megara, Sparta hated Athens enough to side with Corinth. The First Peloponnesian War had begun.

THE PLAGUE OF ATHENS

430–426 BC

The First Peloponnesian War ended with a truce. However, by 431 BC, the truce had ended and the two city-states were very much at war with each other once more. Pericles took the Athenian people inside the walls of the city, hoping to be able to wait long enough for their navy to defeat the armies of the Spartans. This meant a lot of people who usually lived out in the countryside now moved into Athens, which was already a crowded city.

In 430 BC, a terrible disease spread quickly through the crowded city. It was known as the Plague of Athens. People suffered terribly, and the disease killed over 30,000 people, including soldiers, sailors, and Pericles himself. This meant there weren't many people left to fight the war against Sparta.

14

I'M THUCYDIDES. I'M A FAMOUS HISTORIAN, DID YOU KNOW? I WAS IN ATHENS WHEN THE PLAGUE HIT. OH, IT WAS PRETTY TERRIBLE. PEOPLE GOT VERY HOT, THEN THEIR EYES TURNED RED, THEY SNEEZED AND COUGHED, VOMITED, AND HAD VIOLENT <u>CONVULSIONS</u>. SOME PEOPLE COULDN'T STAND TO WEAR CLOTHES, OR THEY NEEDED TO SIT IN COLD WATER. MOST PEOPLE WHO GOT IT DIED WITHIN A WEEK. EVEN THE BIRDS WERE GETTING IT!

Marino Branch
Brainse Marino
Tel: 8336297

THIS IS MYRTIS. SHE WAS AN 11-YEAR-OLD GIRL WHO LIVED IN ATHENS AND DIED DURING THE PLAGUE. THOUSANDS OF YEARS LATER, ARCHAEOLOGISTS FOUND HER BONES. THEY WERE ABLE TO <u>RECONSTRUCT</u> HER FACE TO SHOW US WHAT SHE WOULD HAVE LOOKED LIKE.

THIS PAINTING SHOWS WHAT THE PLAGUE OF ATHENS MIGHT HAVE LOOKED LIKE.

ARE YOU OK?

BLEARCH!

WAIT, WHAT?
TO PRONOUNCE THIS WORD, SAY:

THUCYDIDES = THOO-SID-ID-EEZ

15

THE AGE OF SPARTA

VICTORY... AND HONOUR

Athens was doing badly in the war. When the war had begun, Athens had the better navy and Sparta had the better army, but in recent years Sparta had been building up its strength at sea too. In 405 BC, in a place called the Hellespont, Sparta beat the Athenian navy – only a handful of the 180 Athenian ships survived.

AND DON'T COME BACK! YEAH!

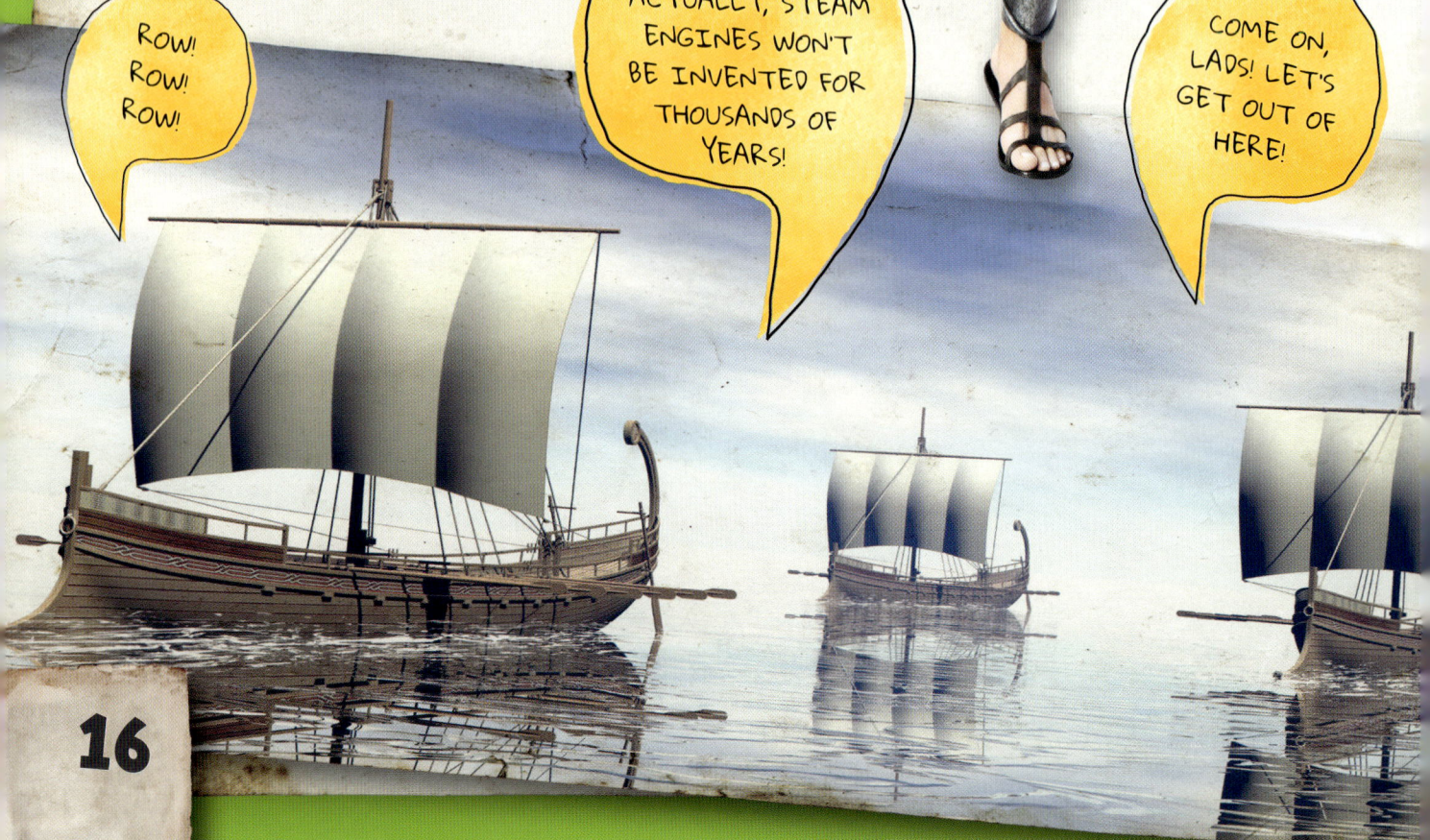

ROW! ROW! ROW!

FULL STEAM AHEAD! WELL, ACTUALLY, STEAM ENGINES WON'T BE INVENTED FOR THOUSANDS OF YEARS!

COME ON, LADS! LET'S GET OUT OF HERE!

Map labels: MACEDONIA, HELLESPONT, THEBES, PERSIA, CORINTH, ATHENS, SPARTA

This pretty much ended the war. Without ships to defend its seas and ports, or **IMPORT** grain, the Athenians could not defend themselves and were slowly starving in their city. Lysander, the Spartan king, left a force to lay **SIEGE** to the Athenian city, and returned home to celebrate his victory.

COME ON, LADS! YOU LOT SIT HERE AND DON'T LET ANYONE IN OR OUT OF THAT CITY, DO YOU HEAR ME? NO FOOD, NO PEOPLE, NO ANIMALS AND ESPECIALLY NO WEAPONS! I'M OFF HOME TO CELEBRATE MY GREAT GLORY. SHOULDN'T TAKE LONG - THEY MIGHT BE THE BEST THINKERS IN THE WORLD, BUT THEY CAN'T EAT POETRY, CAN THEY? WON'T TAKE THEM LONG TO GIVE UP, IF THEY'RE AS CLEVER AS THEY SAY THEY ARE. FOR SPARTAAAAAAAA!!!

Finally, in 404 BC, Athens was forced to give up, and the war was over. Sparta had won.

Could this be the beginning of the end for the ancient Greeks?

PHILLIP OF MACEDON

WHILE YOU WERE FIGHTING...

You might think that meant Greece was now one united country under Spartan rule, but you'd be very wrong. The city-states carried on fighting minor wars against each other. But while all these wars had been going on, a kingdom to the North of Greece, Macedonia, had been growing stronger under its new king, Phillip II of Macedon. Well, we know by now that the Greek city-states didn't like it when the others got too powerful...

RIGHT. I GOT RID OF ALL THE OLD ARMY EQUIPMENT AND GOT EVERYONE NEW HELMETS AND LONGER SPEARS. THIS SHOULD SHOW THOSE ATHENIANS AND THE REST OF THE GREEKS THAT MACEDONIA IS NOW AN IMPORTANT POWER. IN FACT, WE'VE BEEN SLOWLY EXPANDING OUR EMPIRE FOR A WHILE NOW...

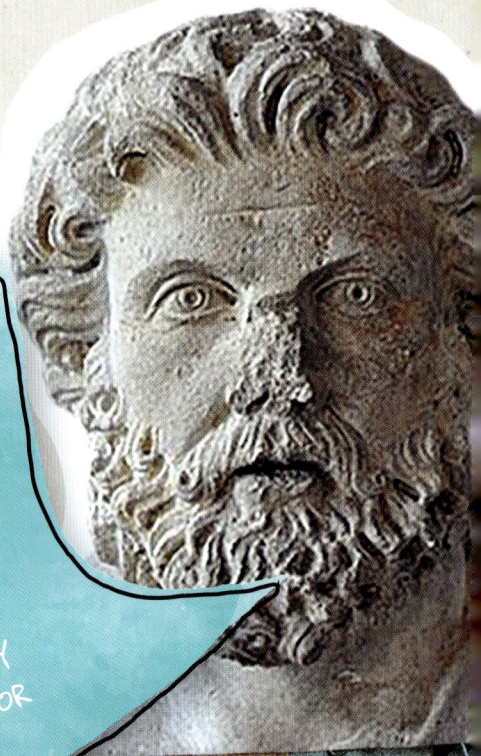

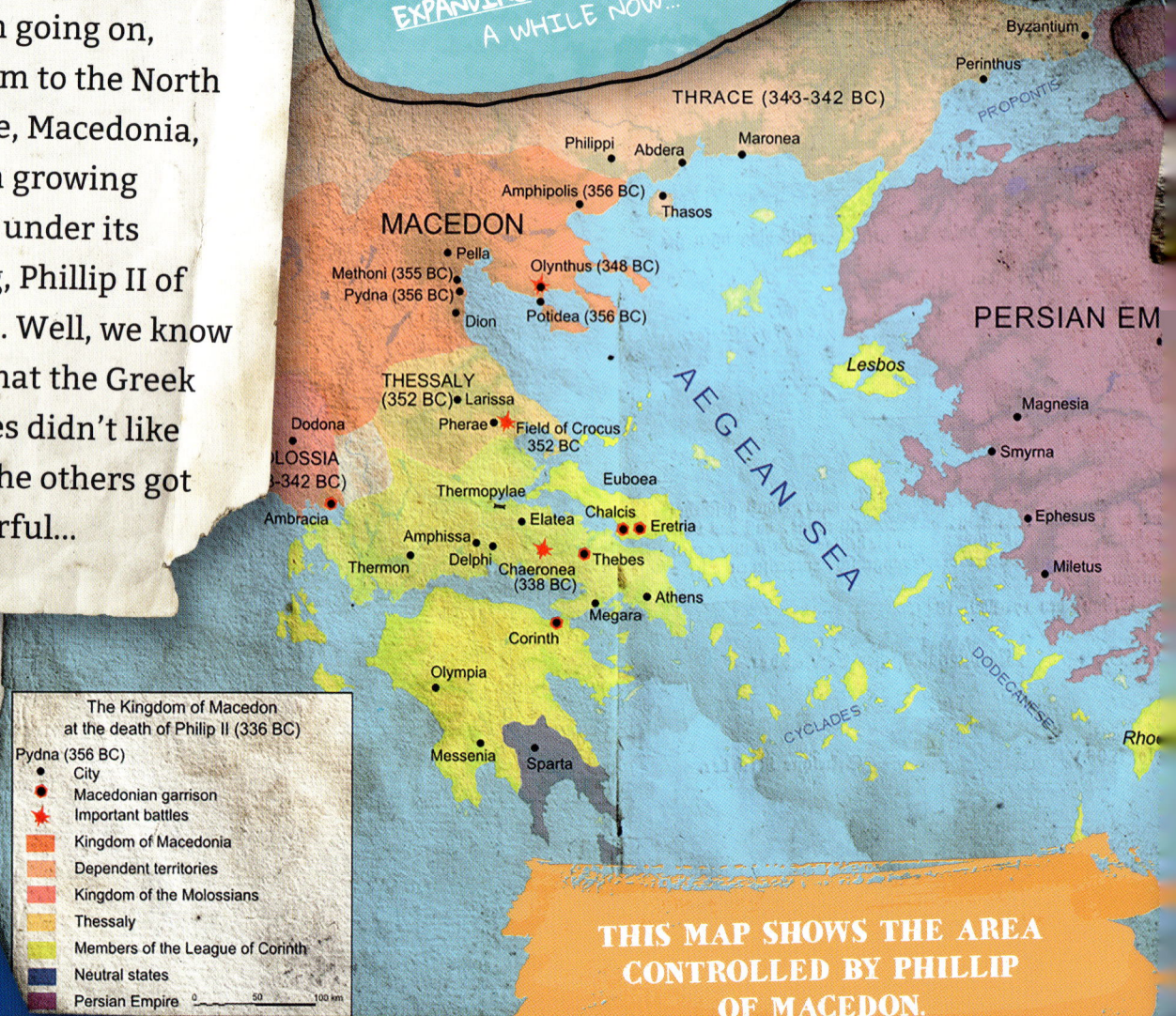

Byzantium
Perinthus
PROPONTIS

THRACE (343-342 BC)

Philippi   Abdera   Maronea
Amphipolis (356 BC)
MACEDON   Thasos
          Pella
Methoni (355 BC)   Olynthus (348 BC)
Pydna (356 BC)   Potidea (356 BC)
          Dion

PERSIAN EM

Lesbos
Magnesia

THESSALY
(352 BC) Larissa
Dodona   Smyrna
      Pherae   Field of Crocus
                352 BC
OLOSSIA
(-342 BC)   AEGEAN SEA
          Thermopylae   Euboea
Ambracia   Chalcis
        Amphissa   Elatea Eretria   Ephesus
Thermon Delphi   Thebes
              Chaeronea   Miletus
              (338 BC) Athens
                  Megara
              Corinth

Olympia   DODECANESE

                  CYCLADES
Messenia   Sparta   Rho

The Kingdom of Macedon
at the death of Philip II (336 BC)
Pydna (356 BC)
      • City
      • Macedonian garrison
      ★ Important battles
      Kingdom of Macedonia
      Dependent territories
      Kingdom of the Molossians
      Thessaly
      Members of the League of Corinth
      Neutral states
      Persian Empire   0   50   100 km

18

THIS MAP SHOWS THE AREA CONTROLLED BY PHILLIP OF MACEDON.